Cracking, Si

and Bubbling Over

Written by Marilyn Woolley

Series Consultant: Linda Hoyt

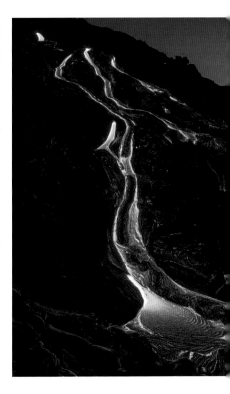

WorldWise™
Content-based Learning

Contents

Introduction

The earth is not one big solid rock – it is made up of plates of rock that fit together like pieces of a jigsaw puzzle. These plates are constantly moving and sometimes crash into each other, or they drift apart from one another.

When this happens, the earth can shake and crack open, or boiling rock can bubble up through the cracks.

At other times large holes open up on the earth's surface.

This happens because water under the ground has pushed up through rock. The soil above the rock has become soft and wet and has fallen away to make a hole.

The blue lines on this map show the earth's plates.

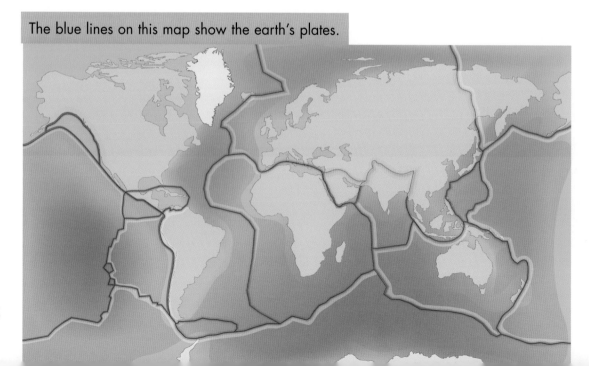

Chapter 1

When the earth cracks open

Earthquakes

If the earth's rocky **plates** crash into one another, the earth moves. Sometimes, it can cause a shake called a small earth **tremor**. At other times, the tremor is so powerful that the ground splits open in big, wide cracks. This is an earthquake.

Did you know?
Scientists use equipment to measure how powerful an earthquake is. The number given to the earthquake shows how strong the earthquake is.

6

Earthquakes can cause landslides. Rocks, soil and
mud can come crashing down hills and destroy
everything in their way. Buildings can topple over
or be crushed.

After an earthquake there can be other tremors,
called aftershocks, that cause more landslides and
cracks in the land.

Earthquakes under the sea

Sometimes, an earthquake can happen under the sea, and a strong, high wall of seawater can quickly rise up and crash onto the shore. This is called a **tsunami**.

The water in a tsunami is like a huge wave that floods over the land and sweeps away houses, buildings, and cars. After the first wave, another wave arrives. And then another. Many people may drown in a tsunami.

Did you know?

The wall of water in a tsunami can be as high as a ten-storey building. It can travel at 800 kilometres an hour.

Chapter 2

When parts of the earth sink

Sinkholes

Sometimes, large pieces of land can fall away or drop and make **sinkholes**. This happens when water under the ground pushes through rock and makes the soil soft and wet. The water then rises up closer to the surface. The ground gets weaker and caves in.

Sinkholes can happen quickly and swallow up cars, roads, or buildings.

THE NEWS

4 May 2018

Early Morning Surprise for Farmer near Rotorua, NZ

Last Tuesday, Colin Tremain, a dairy farmer, got a big surprise when he was rounding up his cows. He saw a huge sinkhole in his paddock. This hole was about 200 metres long and 20 metres deep, big enough to swallow up a six-storey building.

Brad Scott, a volcano scientist, is studying this amazing sinkhole. He said that rainfall over many years had slowly eroded limestone rock under the ground, and the topsoil suddenly collapsed.

This sinkhole happened in Russia. It was nearly 32 metres wide.

Did you know?

Underground stormwater drains and **sewer** pipes can burst or leak lots of water. This underground water can cause sinkholes, too.

Sinking city buildings

Sinking earth can also happen slowly. If tall buildings in cities are built on soil that is over lots of underground water, they can sink, lean or fall over.

Think about

If you dig under wet sand or mud, water will come up and the mud or sand on top will sink down. You have made a sinkhole.

A leaning tower in China

The Leaning Tower of Pisa

Chapter 3

When boiling rock erupts

Under the earth's crust is a layer of very hot rock – so hot that it melts into a liquid. This liquid rock makes bubbles that get bigger and bigger.

If there are cracks in the earth's rocky **plates**, the boiling liquid rock bubbles up and explodes through these cracks. When this happens, the hot rock is called **lava**, and it flows over the land.

Lava is so hot, it can burn anything in its path, but it does cool down and become hard rock. It makes a mountain called a volcano. We know that there are more than 80 volcanoes under the sea. The tops of some of these volcanoes become islands.

When boiling rock erupts

There are more than 1,500 active volcanoes on Earth and many are found within the Pacific Ring of Fire.

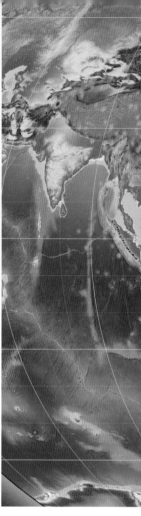

Mount Bromo is an active volcano in Indonesia.

The Pacific Ring of Fire

Mount Ruapehu in New Zealand is an active volcano.

Mount Fuji, Japan

When volcanoes keep erupting, they are called active. Some have not erupted for many years so these are known as sleeping or **dormant** volcanoes.

Conclusion

The earth beneath our feet feels safe and stable. But, in fact, the surface of the earth is always changing. It slides, cracks, sinks and explodes.

This movement and motion can change the environment and wreak havoc on people's lives.

Glossary

dormant not doing anything at this time

emerged came into view; appeared

lava melted rock that comes out of a volcano

plates large pieces of the earth's surface

sewer a drain that carries water and waste

sinkhole a hole in the ground made when soil is washed away by underground water

tremor a shaking movement of the earth

tsunami a huge wave created by an earthquake or volcano under the sea

Index